TAXES

BEGINNERS GUIDE TO UNDERSTANDING TAXES AND WHY WE PAY THEM

By:

Louis McDaniel

FREE BONUS: "Click The Link Below To Receive Your Bonus

https://publishfs.leadpages.co/pangea-health/

CONTENTS

CONCLUSION

INTRODUCTION

Thank you for downloading my book *"Taxes: Beginners Guide To Understanding Taxes And Why We Pay Them."* If you are like most people, you have been paying taxes since you began working and just accepted it as part of life. However, since you downloaded this book, you are probably no longer willing just to accept it as part of life and have become curious to exactly why we pay taxes and what happens to all the money that we pay to our government.

This book has been designed to answer all your tax related questions. From where taxes originated, how the tax rates have changed and who pays taxes to how corporate taxes work and what the federal and state governments do with all that money, this book is going to cover it all

This book will also include why some people pay more taxes than others, and how it is decided who should have to pay how much. This book is also going to cover different things you can do throughout the year to help minimize the amount of taxes you are going to pay and contribute to ensuring that you are getting a refund from the IRS after you file your taxes instead of being required to pay the difference because your automatic deductions were too small. Finally, this book is going to look at the (not very popular) Taxpayer's Bill of Rights, and how they benefit you.

The tax laws in the United States are complicated and change depending on your individual situation. However, it is my hope that when you have finished reading this book all your questions about the United States taxation system will be answered, including questions that you didn't know you had. After reading this book, you should feel more confident heading into a new tax year.

CHAPTER 1

WHAT ARE TAXES AND WHERE DID THEY COME FROM?

Before we can jump right into the history of taxes in the United States and where that money goes, we first need to understand what taxes are and why we are required to pay them. Don't worry if you feel overwhelmed and confused when you are done reading this chapter, everything is going to become clear as we progress through the book, and by the end, you are going to have a good grasp on taxes. This chapter is going to set the groundwork for the rest of the information you are going to read, without it, nothing in the rest of the book is going to make sense to you. When you have finished reading the entire book, come back and read this chapter again, you will probably find that it all makes a lot more sense.

What Are Taxes

The word tax is defined as being a compulsory contribution to state and federal revenue that is levied by the government. It is applied to a worker's income, business profits, and added to the cost of some goods and services and onto some transactions. In fact, if you look at any pay stub or receipt that you have in your house, you are going to see a spot where you were charged taxes.

In the United States, we use something that is called a progressive tax system. What this means is that higher income individuals and corporations are taxed at a higher rate than lower income individual earners. While this means that those who are making less money can keep more of their money, it also complicates the matter of taxes when trying to establish who is responsible for paying what. Later in this book, we are going to look at how tax rates change based on how much you make, and how the more you make, the more you are going to pay your taxes.

Where Did Taxes Come From

The history of taxes in the United States is, surprisingly, pretty interesting. The first income tax suggested was during the War of 1812. The idea was based on the concept of taxes that applied to the British Tax Act of 1798. The British Tax Act essentially stated that a progressive tax rate was applied to everyone's income, and the United States developed a similar proposal in 1814. However, since the treaty of Ghent was signed in 1815, effectively ending hostilities as well as the need for additional revenue, the tax wasn't imposed, and was forgotten about for a while.

In 1861, Congress implemented its first personal income tax to help pay for its war effort in the American Civil War. The Revenue Act of 1861 stated that all incomes of over $800 USD were required to pay 3%. In 1862 this tax was repealed and replaced with another tax.

The Wilson-Gorman Tariff was passed in 1894 by Congress. This was the first ever peacetime tax. It was a tax of 2% on any income over $4000, which meant that less than 10% of households were going to be paying taxes. The purpose was simply to make up for the revenue that was being lost due to tariff reductions. To comply with the act, the New York-based Farmer's Loan & Trust Company announced to its clients that it would pay the tax as well as provide the names for whom the company was acting for, to the collector of internal revenue in the Department of the Treasury, which made them liable for being taxed under the Act.

Among these people was Charles Pollock who was a Massachusetts citizen who owned just ten shares of stock in the Farmer's Loan & Trust Company. He sued the company to prevent the company from paying the tax. On April 8, 1895, a decision was handed down. It was ruled that the taxes imposed on income from property by the Wilson-Gorman Act was unconstitutional. The court treated tax on income from the property to be a direct tax. The Constitution stated that such direct taxes were required to be imposed in proportion to the state's population. Since the tax in question had not been apportioned, it was invalid. After this decision had been reached, the Sixteenth Amendment was proposed and stated that Congress would have the power to collect taxes on any income, regardless of source, and also without regard to census records or any other factors.

From that point, taxes continued to be placed and slowly evolved into being what they are today.

About The IRS

The IRS or Internal Revenue Services has been around since 1862 when President Lincoln and Congress enacted an income tax to pay war expenses. At the time, they were called the Bureau of Internal Revenue. The name was changed to the Internal Revenue Service in the 1950's when the agency was reorganized from an investment structure to one that hired professional employees. The IRS Commissioner and the chief counsel of the IRS are selected by the president and confirmed by the Senate. The IRS was reorganized and modernized in 1998 to resemble a model based on the needs of the private sector.

Essentially the purpose of the IRS is threefold. First, they are expected to collect the appropriate tax revenue with the least amount of cost. Second, they are expected to continually serve the public by through improvement of services and products. Finally, the IRS is to act in a way that ensures the public remains confident in the department's ability to be fair and efficient while maintaining integrity at all levels.

Income Tax Rates Throughout History

The rates that have been charged for taxes has varied throughout history; the top rate has gone from as low as 7% in 1913 to 94% in 1944 and 1945. Here is a brief look at how the rates have varied from 1913 until 2012.

- The top tax rate in 1913 was 7% on incomes that were above $500,000. This amount is equivalent to $12 million today.

- At the time of World War One, the top rate rose to 77% on incomes that were over $1 million dollars. This would be equal to $18.5 million today.

- Top tax rates were reduced in 1921, 1924, 1926, and 1928. In 1928 the top rate was scaled back to 24% for all incomes over $100,000. That is equivalent to $1.38 million today.

- During the Great Depression and World War Two, the income tax rate rose. In 1939, the top rate was 75% and applied to all incomes above $500,000, or $85.1 million today. In 1944 and 1945, the top rate hit an all-time high at 94% applied to all incomes over $200,000 or $2.69 million today.

- During the tax years, 1952 and 1953 the marginal tax rate for individuals was at 92%.

- From 1964 until 2013, the top income tax threshold has been between $200,000 and $400,000. The one exception was between 1981 and 1986 when the top marginal rate was lowered to just 50% for income above $86,000. From 1988 until 1990, the threshold for paying the top rate was even lower with all incomes over $29,750 paying the top rate of 28%.

- In 1992 and 1994 the highest individual tax rates were increased, resulting in a tax increase for all levels of income at a rate of 39.6%.

- In 2004, the top individual income taxes were lowered to 35%. And in 2009, the highest earning 1% of people were required to pay 36.7%.

- In 2012 the two top tax rates were increased to 39.6% and 36% respectively.

This covers only personal taxes. As well as personal taxes, there are also taxes that need to be paid on properties and for businesses. Now that we understand where taxes came from and what they are, we are going to look at who pays taxes and why.

CHAPTER 2

PERSONAL INCOME TAXES

Everyone in the United States pays federal income taxes to the Internal Revenue Services, or IRS, which is a branch of the United States Treasury. Many states also have an additional state income tax, and those that don't are still going to be charging many other types of taxes. In this chapter, we are going to look at the different types of personal taxes you pay in the United States.

A tax year is counted as a calendar year, from January 1 to December 31. You are required to have your federal income tax returns filed by April 15. There is an option to file for an extension which will allow you until August 15 to file your taxes. However, this option does not give you an extension on paying your tax liability, so if you choose to go this route, you are going to have to pay interest on any taxes that were due.

Tax Withholding

You aren't going to be required to pay all of the taxes on your income at one time, thanks to something known as tax withholding. When you are working for someone else, your employer is required to make deductions from your pay. Two of these deductions are federal income tax, and state income tax, if applicable. Your employer is also going to deduct social security, and Medicare contributions. You will know how much your employer has deducted from your pay to put towards your income taxes because they are going to be required to give you a Form W-2 which is a wage and tax statement by January 31.

If you are working for yourself, you are going to have to make quarterly payments of your estimated taxes to the federal and state governments. If you neglect to do this, you are going to have to pay a large penalty as well as interest, in addition to the taxes that you owe.

Progressive Income Tax

In the United States, the income that you pay is called a progressive tax. This means that those who make more money, are required to pay more in taxes than those who make less. Someone who makes very little money is going to be required to pay little to no taxes while someone who makes hundreds of thousands of dollars each year is going to be required to pay more. The tax system was designed this way based on the theory that those who have more money aren't worried about how they are feeding their families and therefore can contribute more to their government.

Tax Brackets

When it comes to figuring out who is going to have to pay what amounts in taxes, the IRS uses something called tax brackets. A tax bracket is a variety of incomes that are taxed at a certain rate. The tax bracket you fall into is going to be determined both by how much you make as well as how you are filing. There are five different filing statuses you can use when you file your taxes.

Single Filing Status – This pertains to you if, on the last day of the year, you were not married or legally separated, and don't fall into another filing status category.

Married Filing Jointly Filing Status – This is applicable when your spouse and yourself agree to file a joint return – your total combined income and deductions are reported.

Married Filing Separately Filing Status – If you and your spouse don't agree to file jointly, you are responsible for your own tax. Occasionally, this method of filing will result in less taxes than filing a joint return.

Head Of Household Filing Status – To qualify for this status, on the last day of the year, you must be (a) unmarried or considered unmarried, (b) you have paid more than half the cost of living for the year, and (c) you have had an eligible person living with you for more than half the year (excluding temporary absences).

Qualifying Widow(er) With Dependent Children Filing Status – That status applies to those who lost a spouse in the last tax year to allow them to still file a joint return.

Here is an example of how tax brackets are determined, based off the 2015 tax brackets.

Single Filers:

10% - Up to $9,225

15% - $9,226 to $37,450

25% - $37,451 to $90,750

28% - $90,751 to $189,300

33% - $189,301 to $411,500

35% - $411,501 to $413,200

39.6% - $413,201 or more

Married, filing jointly or qualifying widow(er)s:

10% - Up to $18,450

15% - $18,451 to $74,900

25% - $74,901 to $151,200

28% - $151,201 to $230,450

33% - $230,451 to $411,500

35% - $411,501 to $464,850

39.6% - $464,851 or more

Married Filing Separately:

10% - Up to $9,225

15% - $9,226 to $37,450

25% - $37,451 to $75,600

28% - $75,601 to $115,225

33% - $115,226 to $205,750

35% - $205,751 to $232,425

39.6% - $262,426 or more

Head Of Household:

10% - Up to $13,150

15% - $13,151 to $50,200

25% - $50,201 to $129,600

28% - $129,601 to $209,850

33% - $209,851 to $411,500

35% - $411,501 to $439,000

39.6% - $439,001 or more

To explain better how this works, we are going to look at two people who both file their taxes in the single bracket and how much tax they are each going to be required to pay. Keep in mind, this isn't taking any potential deductions into consideration, but just their income and how it would be taxed. This will give you a better idea on how those who make more money end up being taxed much higher than those who make less.

<u>Person One</u>: This person makes a total of $31,998 for the year.

On the first $9,225: 9,225 * 10% = $922.50

On the balance of $9,225 to $31,998: $31,998 - $9,225 = $22,773 then $22,773 * 15% = $3,415.95

Which makes their taxes a total of: $922.50 + $3,415.95 = $2,493.45 or 7.79% of their total income.

Person 2: This person makes $248,685 for the year. This person makes a total of $31,998 for the year.

On the first $9,225: 9,225 * 10% = $922.50

On the balance of $9,225 to $37,450: $37,450 - $9,225 = $28,224 then $28,224 * 15% = $4,233.60

On the balance of $37,451 to $90,750: $90,750 - $37,451= $53,299 then $53,299 * 25% = $13,324.75

On the balance of $90,751 to $189,300: $189,300 - $90,751= $98,549 then $98,549 * 28% = $27,593.72

On the balance of $189,301 to $248,685: $248,685 - $189,301= $59,384 then $59,384 * 33% = $19,596.72

Which makes their taxes a total of: $922.50 + $4,233.60 + $13,324.75 + $27,593.72 + $19,596.72 = $65,661.29 or 26.4% of their total income.

As you can see, those who make more money are going to end up paying a significantly higher percentage of their overall income towards their federal income tax. However, this was without any deductions being claimed. When you consider deductions, these numbers are going to change, although, at the end of the day, a person who makes a higher income is going to pay a higher percentage of their income towards taxes, even if it isn't as drastic as the example above makes it seem.

The Capital Gain Loophole

All money that you make during the year is counted as income, regardless of where it comes from and that can throw things off. For example, if you are working at a job for a wage, that is income. If you win the lottery or even find a twenty-dollar bill on the street, those are income as well. There is one exception to this rule. If you buy and sell stocks, or pieces of companies, and make a profit this is considered capital gains and not income. This is how the very wealthy make a lot of their money, by investing. Investing in stocks is a glorified way of gambling when you look at the bare bones of it. You are purchasing pieces of a company in the hopes that the company is going to do well and you will be able to sell the stocks and make money.

If you take one thousand dollars and go to the casino and successfully gamble it and win one hundred thousand dollars, you are going to have to pay income tax on ninety-nine thousand dollars. Now, if you take the same one thousand dollars and buy stocks with it, and then sell the stocks for one hundred thousand dollars, the money you have made from the stocks is not income, but instead capital gain which means that you are only going to end up paying about half the amount of income tax on it.

This isn't the only place where the wealthy is awarded tax breaks. If you are working for a wage and decide that you are going to go out and buy yourself something with your money, you are going to have to pay a sales tax on that purchase. This is true whether it's a can of beer, a car, or a new TV. The tax is going to vary based on what you are buying and where you are buying it, but the point is you are being charged tax. However, when the wealthy use their money to buy and sell pieces of companies, they aren't required to pay a tax on the purchase price.

While these points may make it seem as though the wealthier you are, the fewer taxes you pay, you have to remember that the more personal income you have in a year, the higher your tax rate is. Think about the example we did above. While the wealthy can soften this a little bit, overall they are still contributing more to the government tax pool than someone who makes less money.

Companies are also taxed. However, the tax system for a company is different from individual taxes. We are going to look more in depth at how companies pay their taxes, but first, we are going to take a look at some of the other personal taxes that a person is going to pay outside of their income taxes.

CHAPTER 3

OTHER PERSONAL TAXES

Your income isn't the only thing that you are taxed on in the United States. You are also taxed almost every time you spend any money on anything, as well as anytime you receive money from anywhere. However, these taxes aren't all black and white. There are exemptions and situations that are specific to come from these taxes. Here, we will look at some of the most common taxes in the United States, and what situations they would apply in. If you want any more information on any of these taxes and how they might apply to you, it would be in your best interest to contact an accountant or the IRS directly for more specific information.

Sales Tax – This tax is calculated as a percentage of what you are paying when you purchase a good or a service. Sales taxes vary by state in even by the municipality in some cases. Sales taxes are considered to be regressive, which means that they are applied equally to all consumers based on what they buy. This system leads to lower income households being more affected by the tax. What this means is that people with a lower income often spend a larger proportion of their income to these taxes.

Explaining Regressive Taxes

For example: Imagine there are two individuals in a grocery store and they each purchase $100 in groceries for the week. Each of them pays 7% in tax on the whole amount of their groceries. The first individual makes $2000 that week. That makes the sales tax on their groceries 0.35% of their income. The second individual makes $320 that week. That makes the sales tax on their groceries 2.2% of their income. Even though both people are paying the same sales tax, the person with the lower income is paying a higher percentage of income, which makes the tax regressive.

Property Tax – This tax is typically imposed by your local government and is charged on a recurring basis. Property taxes are imposed on the value of the property, and are typically paid once a year or monthly as part of their mortgage payments. While in some ways property taxes can be considered regressive, it is also not regressive at the same time. If two people were living in the same area, in houses of the same value, but made a significantly different income, it would be regressive since the property taxes would be the same, and the person with the lower income would be paying a higher percentage of their income. However, since people who make less money are often living in homes that are less expensive, their income taxes are going to be lower as well, thereby making it difficult to label property taxes concretely as a regressive tax.

Estate Tax – At first glance this tax seems unfair. Estate taxes are imposed when the owner of a home dies and the property is being transferred to someone else. It was created to prevent the accumulation of tax-free wealth among the country's population that already holds the most wealth. The reason this tax isn't as unfair as it seems at first glance is that the initial $5.43 million of an estate's worth is exempt from this tax. This means that only about one percent of people are affected by this tax since the vast majority of people don't have an estate that is worth more than $5.43 million.

Gift Tax – This tax is similar to that of the estate tax, in that it is a tax that is only implemented when wealth is being transferred from one person to another. All gifts over $14,000 are taxable, with the tax to be paid by the recipient. This tax applies to gifts like company shares or cars as well as cash gifts. It doesn't matter who is gifting the money to you; this tax applies to all gifts. This tax is also regressive; in that, it is going to be applied at the same percentage without taking into consideration what your income in. Due to this, sometimes people might choose to take a cash gift over a luxury car because it is easier to pay the taxes on the gift from the gift money then it is to pay the taxes on a new car from the money you are currently making.

Luxury Tax – The luxury tax is one that is placed on products and services that are deemed to be non-essential or unnecessary. This is an indirect tax that is only incurred by the person who purchases or uses the product. Today's definition of luxury taxes leans more towards "sinful" products such as tobacco, alcohol, and high-end automobiles.

Excise Tax – This tax is based on a quantity of an item instead of an item's overall value. For example, the federal government charges an excise tax on every gallon of fuel that is purchased regardless of how much the seller is charging for that gas.

User Fees – User fees are assessed on a wide variety of services. Some of the most commonly used ones are airline tickets, rental cars, hotel rooms, toll roads and licenses. These taxes are also considered to be a regressive tax since they are the same for everyone, regardless of the amount of income you have.

Payroll Tax – There are two different facets to the payroll tax. One is the Medicare Tax; the other is Social Security tax. Both an employee and an employer needs to pay contributions to the Social Security tax, based on their income levels up to maximum earning. On the other hand, there is no maximum taxable wage on the Medicare Tax. Both of these taxes are considered to be regressive taxes since you are required to pay the same percentage of them regardless of how much money you are making, or at least until you hit the annual wage maximum for the Social Security Tax.

Capital Gain Tax – As we covered previously, the capital gain tax is paid on any profits that are made from the sale of an asset. Profits made from selling real estate are exempt up to $250,000 for single people and $500,000 for those who are married and filing jointly as long as the home was a principal residence for at least two of the last five years.

Now that we understand the different taxes that are applied to individuals, we are going to take a look at corporate taxes and learn how businesses are taxed.

CHAPTER 4

CORPORATE TAXES

We know that companies are taxed differently than citizens are. We also know that when a person earns income, they are taxed on a percentage of their total income, but this doesn't apply the same way to businesses. Businesses are taxed on profit, not on income. This means that anything that is classified as a business expense isn't going to be taxed. This allows giant corporations to get away with making tens of billions of dollars and only paying a small amount of taxes, and in some cases, no taxes at all.

How Are Corporate Tax Laws Created?

You are probably wondering how tax laws that seem so skewed towards those who have large companies and therefore make a lot of money, are created. After all, it seems almost unbelievable that a large business would be able to get away with not paying taxes! The tax laws in the United States are written by Congress, which is the legislative branch of our government. The people who are in Congress get there by being elected by citizens. It takes a lot of money to get into Congress, because campaigning is expensive and if you don't campaign, you aren't going to get the votes you need to become a member of Congress. This means that people who want to get elected to Congress need to raise money to campaign and get elected. The money that is raised is typically raised from people who want Congress to do something for them.

Essentially what happens is that corporations hire people called lobbyists to donate money to those members of Congress who are willing to write the laws in the way most beneficial to them. Although we don't refer to this as a bribe, and everyone acts as though the money that is given to politicians from these corporations has nothing to do with the way they vote, that about sums up what is happening. Doing this can mean that a loophole is written into the legislation that allows your company to have a tax break, although these loopholes are usually written so obscurely that no one can find them in the legislation unless they are looking for them.

For example: Pretend for a minute that you are a company that makes pencils. You create a business group with other pencil makers. You want a way to pay less in taxes. Your business group hires a lobbyist who finds members of Congress who agree with what you want. You donate money to them to fund their election campaigns. When the laws are written, the politicians that you have funded write into the tax code "pencil makers don't have to pay taxes." Of course, it wouldn't be written this way. It would be written into the tax code in 800 words of jam-packed text that never mentions the word pencil. However, it would define the tax law in a way that the only ones who can claim it are you and the other pencil makers. In fact, no one else would even notice those eight hundred words and therefore won't complain about the fact you are getting such a sweet deal.

Types Of Businesses

When you have a business organization, you must register as a specific type of business. The two main types of organizations are Limited Liability Companies (LLCs) or Corporations.

Limited Liability Companies

A limited liability company is not a corporation; you cannot incorporate a business as an LLC. An LLC is also considered to be a "pass-through business." The profits and losses of these companies are passed through the owners and shareholders. This means that the business income is considered to be the owner's or stockholder's income, and the owner or shareholder is thus responsible for paying the tax on his or her personal tax return.

An LLC is formed by one or more business individuals or members. These members file Articles of Organization and set out an operating agreement. The profits and losses of the business are passed on to these members based on their share of the membership.

An LLC is taxed based on the Adjusted Gross Income of the owners of the company. Adjusted Gross Income is the total that is left after you subtract the tax deductions that are allowable from your gross income. The gross income can be reduced by claiming some business expenses, such as supplies, gas mileage, and equipment rental fees.

Corporations

A corporation is a separate legal entity. Unlike an LLC, the profits and losses of the corporation are taxable to the corporation itself and not to the owners or shareholders. A corporation is formed by filing a Corporate Organization and by designating shareholders and a board of directors to oversee the corporate business.

While the members of an LLC are taxed in their portion of all income, owners of a corporation are not paid, but instead receive dividends. They are then taxed on their dividend income, as normal income. The corporation itself, however, is taxed on the profit at the corporate rate.

There are two different types of corporations, and while the above information is true for both, there are also some key differences that you should be aware of. The two types of corporations are called C Corporations and S Corporations. After you have formed your corporation, you can elect S Corporations status with the Internal Revenue Service, provided you meet the requirements of being a domestic corporation with no more than one hundred approved shareholders and only issue one class of stock.

S Corporations

The "s" in S Corporation does not stand for small, even though it is limited to less than one hundred shareholders. It is named for Subchapter S in the Internal Revenue Code. S Corporations offer protection to shareholders from the business's liabilities but allow income to be passed through to the shareholders, who would then pay taxes on it.

How Are C Corporations And S Corporations Taxed Differently?

You become a C Corporation by default if you do not elect to be an S corporation with the IRS. Taxation draws the most definitive line between the two types of corporations.

In a C Corporation, shareholders receive dividends or shares of the corporation's revenue; they can then sell those shares for profit or a loss. Those who own the C Corporation face a twice the tax predicament. The corporation pays taxes on all of its profits, while the owners are taxed an additional amount of the shares that they receive. The owners who work in the business, typically as executives of the company, are also employees and must be paid a salary. This salary is also taxed as personal income.

An S Corporation, on the other hand, does not pay dividends to its owners. Instead, an S Corporation files a tax return that shows its net profit or loss for the year. This amount is then passed through to the individual shareholders and reported on their personal income tax returns, even though it is not received in the form of dividends.

What Are The Benefits Of Being An S Corporation?

An S Corporation is still a corporation. That means that it retains the separate entity protection of a corporation, as well as the corporate cover to be protected from liabilities. This means that the owners are safe from lawsuits as well as the debts of the corporation.

While owners of sole proprietorships and partnerships are required to pay self-employment tax on total profits, an S Corporation has its profits reduced by the amount that is paid to owners as employees and therefore the self-employment tax bill for the S Corporation is lower.

An S Corp is also going to be able to avoid the double taxation that a C Corporation gets. Instead of paying taxes on its profits and then having the owners taxed on the dividends, an S Corporation won't have to pay income tax; the owner's simply pay taxes on their share of the profits.

When an S Corp loses money, each owner's share of that loss is passed through to their individual income tax return. This loss can reduce all or part of any other income an owner has.

Understanding how different businesses are taxed becomes even more complicated when you consider that an LLC has the option of being taxed as an LLC, a C Corporation or an S Corporation. Of course, they must meet the eligibility but imagine if you had the option to change how you were being taxed to benefit you and allow you to pay the least amount of taxes as possible.

CHAPTER 5

WHERE DOES ALL THIS TAX MONEY GO?

Now that we know that everyone pays taxes and that when you earn more money, you pay more taxes, let's have a look at where all of these tax dollars are going. Since there are both Federal and State taxes, we are going to look at the two different taxes separately.

Federal Taxes

If you were to ask the American people what percentage of their tax dollars are allocated where, they are going to have assumptions, but those assumptions are nowhere near where the money is going.

The federal government budget is broken down into discretionary spending and mandatory spending. For the purpose of this breakdown, we are going to compare the two categories and look at the federal budget as a whole.

Health – The largest amount of your tax dollars is going to fund health care in the United States. This goes towards health care initiatives such as Medicare, Medicaid and the Children's Health Care Program and is responsible for 28 cents of every federal tax dollar.

Social Security – The second largest amount of your tax dollar goes towards funding Social Security. This covers the next 25.3 cents of every federal tax dollar.

Military – The third largest amount of your tax dollar is allocated for Defense and Homeland Security. This makes up 16.2 cents of every federal tax dollar. This includes paying for the current war and military as well as interest on the military debt.

Agriculture, Commerce & Transportation – 8 cents of every federal income tax dollar is going towards agriculture and transportation spending.

Veterans – 4 cents of every federal tax dollar that is paid goes towards supporting our veterans. This can mean support with health care, mental health services as well as housing and financial aid.

Social Services – Education, training and social services receive 4.3 cents of every income tax dollar. This money goes towards paying for elementary, secondary and higher education, as well as other beneficiaries such as employment training centers.

International Affairs – One of the smallest amounts of your tax dollar, 2 cents go to foreign affairs. This includes humanitarian assistance, international financial programs, and conduct of foreign affairs.

Environment, Energy And Science – Environmental programs, energy explorations and any other programs that are related to general science, technology and space are allocated 2 cents of each income tax dollar.

Housing And Community Development – 1.1 cents of each income tax dollar is spent on housing assistance as well as community development programs.

Other – If you add up the numbers above, you will notice that there are 9.1 cents of your dollar missing. This amount covers things like the legislative branch, judicial branch, independent agencies and departments of Commerce, Interior, and Treasury, as well as interest on nonmilitary debts.

Keep in mind that these are the reported allocations from 2008, and the numbers are going to be a little different than this. Also, that 1.1 cents that are being put towards housing and community development translates into a significant amount of money, and doesn't include the money that is also taken from state taxes. However, this gives you a good snapshot of what is being done with your Federal Income taxes.

State Taxes

When we are considering where our state taxes are going, it is important to be aware that it varies from state to state. The numbers we are going to look at below are based on the average of all states in the year 2013. These figures are also not taking the federal funds that the states also spend in a year. This is simply looking at the average of where your State Taxes are going across the country.

Education Spending – On average, each state spends about 25% of their overall spending on public kindergarten to grade twelve educations. Typically, a state will allocate education expenditures to local school districts to be distributed instead of paying the expenses directly. An additional thirteen percent of state expenditures are used to fund higher education, including community colleges, vocational institutions, and university systems. That means that out of each dollar that goes towards your state taxes, a total of around thirty-eight cents is going to education in some way.

Health Care Allocation – After education, the next largest expenditure that the state pays are on health programs. This is primarily used to fund Medicaid and Children's Health Insurance Program, also known as CHIP. In an average month, more than 45 million children, parents, elderly, and disabled people benefit from these programs. Overall, about sixteen cents of every dollar you pay into state taxes goes into health care.

Transportation Expenses – State transportation expenses include those for public transportation systems, infrastructure spending, and road and bridge repairs. On average, each state pays about five percent of their expenditures are going to fund transportation services or about five cents of every state tax dollar.

Corrections Facilities – This category doesn't cover just state prison costs. It also covers juvenile justice programs and parole programs. Corrections costs make up about four percent of state expenditures, which means about four cents of every dollar that you pay your state taxes.

Low Income Assistance – About one percent of state spending is allocated towards helping those who make a low income. Low-income assistance programs include both the Temporary Assistance for Needy Families program as well as general assistance that is given to low-income health care programs.

That means that a mere one cent of every dollar you pay towards state taxes is put towards low-income assistance programs.

Additional Programs – The last thirty-five cents of every state dollar you pay is divided up into many different additional programs. Some of these programs include:

- Care for residents with disabilities

- Economic development

- Environmental programs

- Expenditures for state police

- General aid to local governments

- Health benefits for public employees

- Parks and Recreation

- Pensions

As we stated before, these numbers are based on the average across all of the states. In some cases, the variations of spending are pretty significant. For example, Vermont spends thirty-two percent of its budget on kindergarten to grade twelve educations, while West Virginia only spends ten percent on the same category. Similarly, Missouri puts about thirty-six percent of its budget into Medicaid while Wyoming puts seven percent.

CHAPTER 6

GETTING READY TO FILE YOUR
PERSONAL INCOME TAXES

For many people, the payments that are made throughout the year to their federal income taxes are made automatically on their behalf by their employers. Your employer must report your total income and withheld taxes that you have paid by submitting a form call a W-2 to the IRS. When you file your taxes, you are going to be told what the total number is that you owe and whether that number is more or less than you have already paid throughout the year. When you have paid less than you owe, you are going to be required to pay the difference. However, when you pay more than what you owe, you will be entitled to a refund. To help you ensure that you are that you don't owe the IRS money at tax time, there are things you can do throughout the year. In this chapter, we are going to look at some of the things you can do to prepare for doing your taxes.

Get Organized – Any financial expert will tell you that the most important thing for you to do is be organized about your finances. You can use personal finance software to help you maintain accurate records. Keep records of your expenses, such as mileage expenses that were incurred for business purposes, and get receipts for your charitable contributions. It is also essential that you keep accurate records of any stocks that you purchase and sell as well as your stock options. This is by far the most important thing to remember when it comes to being ready to do your taxes. The last thing you want is to realize that you are missing an important piece of paperwork after you have submitted your taxes, and need to file them again or end up owing more than you should because you overlooked something.

Contribute To Your 401 (k) – When you contribute the maximum to your 401 (k) retirement plan, you are going to be able to defer the taxes that you paid on your contributions. This also allows your contributions to increase through compound interest.

Adjust Your Withholding – Your withholding is the amount of money that your employer is taking from your pay to put towards your taxes. If your marital status has changed, or if you are in a different tax bracket than you were in the previous tax year, you should ask your employer to adjust what they are taking from you. If sufficient taxes are not being taken from your paycheck, or if you are self-employed, it is recommended that you make estimated tax payments to the appropriate tax authority to avoid year-end penalties.

Contribute To Your IRA – Your IRA is an individual retirement account. It is important to contribute to your IRA as early as possible in the year to take advantage of compound interest. Another advantage to putting money into your IRA is that is that in most cases, contributions to your IRA are tax deductible.

Consider Tax Efficient Investments – There are some investments that are better to make over others. Some examples of tax efficient investments include tax-free municipal bonds and tax-efficient mutual funds. These investments will help you minimize the amount of taxes that you are going to have to pay at the end of the year.

Make Charitable Donations – The actual amount of money that you contribute to a charity is eligible to be deducted from the amount of income that is being taxed. Pledging an amount isn't enough to earn the deduction, only the amount that was given to the charity.

Ensure The IRS Has Your Address Right – Every year, the IRS reports that there are tens of thousands of refunds that cannot be delivered because of bad addresses. Not only will the wrong address mean that you aren't able to get your refund, but you could also be missing out on other important communications from the IRS.

Ultimately, the most important thing to ensuring that you aren't left owing money after your taxes are filed is being organized and prepared. Being prepared means that you aren't scrambling around on April 14, trying to get all of your papers together to get your taxes filed before the deadline.

How To File Your Taxes

When you are ready to file your taxes, there are different ways you can go about it. You can choose to do your taxes yourself, or you can hire someone to do your taxes on your behalf. There are advantages to both ways.

When you choose to do your taxes, you are going to be able to file them free of charge. You can do this with blank forms that you can get from the IRS and submit them either online or through the mail.

Another way to do them yourself, although it isn't free, is to purchase tax preparation software. The advantage to this is that while you are paying for the software, it will ensure that you don't miss anything. Income tax preparation software works by walking you through the income tax process, asking you questions and making sure nothing is missed. Another advantage of this process is that if you have forgotten to have something on hand, you can stop the process and come back to it.

If you choose to hire someone to do your taxes on your behalf, you are paying for their expertise. There is a lower chance of there being mistakes on your income tax return, although if you have forgotten to bring something with you to your appointment, you might find yourself being charged an additional fee to make a second appointment.

Filing Your Taxes When You Are Living Abroad

If you are a US citizen who is living in another country, the regulations for filing taxes from income on estates, earned income and gifts still apply, as well as paying estimated taxes are the same for you as they are for someone who is living in the United States.

If you are being paid in a currency other than US dollars, you must convert those amounts on your income tax return to US dollars. Taxpayers use the yearly average exchange rate to report foreign-earned income that was regularly received throughout the year. However, if you made foreign transactions on specific days when the rates may have been different, you can also convert by using the exchange rates applicable on those exact days.

If you are a US citizen but live overseas, or you are in the military stationed outside of the US, you are automatically granted a two-month extension on the filing date and the due date of any taxes you may have to pay. If for any other reason, you are unable to file your return before the automatic two-month extension, you can request an additional extension by submitting Form 4868 before the two-month extension date. Even if you are granted these extensions, you are still obligated to pay interest on any unpaid tax accrued from the original due date of the return.

Ensuring that you are prepared to file your taxes correctly is an important step in making sure that you aren't going to end up paying more than your fair share of taxes. Your specific tax situation is going to be different than your neighbors to make sure that you know about any tax laws and exceptions that might pertain to you and your individual situation.

CHAPTER 7

TAXPAYER'S BILL OF RIGHTS

Many people aren't aware, but each and every taxpayer in the United States has a set of fundamental rights that are in place to protect them when they are dealing with the IRS. In this chapter, we are going to briefly explain each of the ten fundamental rights of American taxpayers.

1. The Right To Be Informed – Taxpayers, have the right to be informed on what is expected of them and what they need to do to comply with the tax laws. They are entitled to clear explanations of all laws and IRS procedures in all tax forms, publications, notices, correspondence, and instructions. Taxpayers also have the right to be informed of all IRS decisions

regarding their tax accounts as well as receive explanations of the outcomes that are clear and concise.

2. The Right To Quality Service – When taxpayers have dealings with the IRS, they have the right to receive courteous, prompt, and profession assistance. They should be spoken to in a way that is easily understood and is entitled to speak to a supervisor regarding any inadequate service.

3. The Right To Pay No More Than The Correct Amount Of Tax – Taxpayers have the right to pay only the amount of tax that is legally due, including interest and penalties. They also have the right to have the IRS apply for all tax payments correctly.

4. The Right To Challenge The IRS's Position And Be Heard – Taxpayers have the right to raise objections and provide additional documentation in response to the IRS and expect that the IRS will consider their timely objections and documentation promptly and fairly. They are also entitled to receive a response regardless of whether the IRS agrees with their position.

5. The Right To Appeal An IRS Decision In An Independent Forum – Taxpayers are entitled to a fair and impartial

administrative appeal of most IRS decisions. They also have the right to a written response regarding the decision of the Office of Appeals. Taxpayers also have the right to take their cases to court.

6. The Right To Finality – Taxpayers have the right now know how much time they have to challenge the decisions of the IRS as well as how long the IRS has to audit a particular tax year or to collect a tax debt. Taxpayers are entitled to know when the IRS has completed an audit.

7. The Right To Privacy – Taxpayers have a right to expect that any dealings with the IRS will comply with the law and not be any more intrusive than is necessary. This includes any IRS inquiry, examination, and enforcement action.

8. The Right To Confidentiality – Taxpayers have the right to expect that any and all information that they provide to the IRS will be kept confidential unless authorized by the taxpayer or the law. Taxpayers also have the right to expect that the appropriate action will be taken against anyone who wrongfully uses or discloses taxpayer return information.

9. The Right To Retain Representation – Taxpayers have the right to retain an authorized representative of their choice to represent them in their dealings with the IRS. If they are unable to afford representation, they have the right to seek assistance from the Low Income Taxpayer Clinic.

10. The Right To A Fair And Just Tax System – Taxpayers have the right to expect the tax system to consider facts and circumstances that might affect their ability to pay or provide timely information. Taxpayers also have the right to receive assistance from the Taxpayer Advocate Service if the IRS has not resolved their tax issues properly or if they are experiencing financial difficulty. (IRS.gov)

Understanding what rights you have and what you are entitled to when it comes to your dealings with the IRS can go a long way towards making your dealings easier and less stressful. There is no reason to fear the IRS; they are bound by rules, and they are required to explain everything to you in a way that you understand it. Many people are confused by the tax system; this is not necessary. You are entitled to understand how the tax system works, and there are people in place to ensure that you do.

CHAPTER 8

BASICS OF FILING

If you have reached the phase in your life when you are required to file for taxes, then, first of all, welcome to the world of the tax-paying adult and all the responsibilities that follow. Filing taxes is not as intimidating as one might think, so we are going to break the ice for you and share some valuable information about tax filing.

In order to start filing your taxes, first get a W2 form from your employer. This sheet or form reveals to the IRS what you do, your income status, and most importantly, how much you paid in taxes. Please note that this form has to be requested and collected from your place of work, and if you do not ask for it yourself, the company or employer might never get it to you, since they are under no legal obligation to do so. Even if you have changed multiple jobs throughout the year, you still must get a W2 form from all employers.

The 1098-E Form is the most dreaded for former students. Namely, this form is aimed at paying back your student loan. If you have paid on your student loan, that amount will be written off from the total student loan amount. In order to be exempted from additional $4,000 of the student loan for educational expenses, get a tuition receipt.

The 1040EZ, 1040, & 1040A Tax Forms for electronic filing became one of the most popular ways to file taxes. They are efficient and fast, and remove the bother of hard copy forms. Many websites offer free tax filing, including IRS' website.

What many taxpayers are looking forward to throughout the year is filing for both federal and state tax income returns, because they bring some extra bucks back that are sometimes forgotten about..

Filing Status - What Form to File?

A filing status is very important to determine since it, according to Tax law, defines filing requirements, extended and standard deductions, tax brackets, etc. It also contributes to defining the threshold for Social Security taxation.

Your status has to be known to the IRS since the whole system roughly relies on how much an individual or a family can put aside for taxes. According to this theory, as a single person, you are able to support the budget a bit more than someone with children, so your tax percentage will be higher, sincesince you do not have any children dependent on your wages. Joint filing is allowed for married couples only, which facilitates the whole process and administration.

There are five statuses according to which taxes can be filed. They are:

<u>Head of the Household</u> status can be claimed by single, unmarried US citizens or residents who have been living in the USA for at least 12 months. They must solely bore more than a half of the household- maintenance costs. Also, a head of the household must offer proof that they have provided for a family member, like child, parent, or relative, amounting to more than 50%. The persons you provided for must be registered to be living with you for the last 6 months by the date of submission, except for parents.

The relative or/and child must be legally related to you if you are about to list them as dependents. This excludes partners and their children, even if you provide more than 50% of support for them.

The IRS cuts you some slack by not deducting days for extenuating circumstances during the child's absence for reasons including a vacation or spending time with the other parent if you are divorced or separated, as long as it is in line with the custody agreement. If another dependent, e.g. relative, dies before the end of the tax year, you can still claim the head of the household status if you met the requirements.

Household expenses are also defined by the law and include general costs that concern the household, including house repairs, mortgage, rent, estate insurance, domestic help, and food. Excluded expenses are defined as individual costs like education and medical costs, as well as clothing, vacation, life insurance costs, and all forms of transport.

Single Status is the least favorable position you can have when it comes to paying taxes. A single person is defined as an unmarried, divorced or legally separated. This category of people is subjected to the highest tax rates. The single status may take other definitions under different federal laws.

Married Status- File Jointly or Individually

For spouses who live in a separate estate, it is better to file a joint tax form since it lowers the taxes if one spouse earns more than half of the incomes. If spouses make equal income amounts or if they live in community property states, then filing separately may lower taxes more. It is easy to calculate. The main shortage of filing separately is that both spouses have to claim the standard deduction, and neithercan claim college tuition or interest deduction on a student loan.

If one spouse is unemployed or earns little, then the other spouse can ask for a deduction on account of a nonworking spouse. Joint tax return file is only possible if spouses' tax year starts on the same day, they are still married by the day of submission, and if neither is a foreigner with no clear residency status. Also, if the foreigner spouse is earning incomes outside the USA, it is advised to file separate tax returns, since other incomes earned abroad would be subject to US taxation.

Filing a joint return makes both spouses liable for unpaid taxes and penalties regardless of which spouse is to blame. Still, joint liability can be circumvented if you did not know that the spouse had unpaid taxes. Spouses may also ask for a separation of liability.

CHAPTER 9

WHAT HAS TO BE REPORTED AS INCOME?

Let us first be clear of which incomes are taxable. There are two categories of incomes which can be subject to taxes, which are incomes that you earned and incomes that you don't earn. Earned incomes encompass salaries, wages, tips, bonuses, sick pay, unemployment benefits, commissions, and certain noncash fringe benefits.

Unearned incomes include interest, profit from the sale of estates, dividends, rents, royalties, winnings from games of chance, alimony, and business and farm incomes.

In some situations, you can be exempted from tax payment. The taxation of an individual depends on their gross income, so when defining your income, you have to report all taxable income, including taxable scholarships. Non-taxable scholarships do not to be listed since they are not liable to taxation and serve educational purposes. Your scholarship is taxable when in the form of a paycheck in exchange for tutoring, research teaching, and other services you might enjoy under the scholarship. It is referred to as study-work income.

Fringe Benefits

Fringe benefits include services and other perks which the employer pays for an employee, e.g. transportation. Fringe benefits are usually taxable unless stated otherwise by law. A cafeteria plan represents a list of benefits provided by your employer that you would like to receive instead of cash. A cafeteria plan includes: accident benefits and health benefits (but, be careful, since the Archer medical savings accounts (Archer MSAs) or long-term care insurance is not part of the deal), adoption assistance, dependent care assistance, health savings accounts, group term life insurance payments (along with costs that cannot be excluded from salaries).

Benefits which cannot qualify as cafeteria plan benefits are Archer medical savings accounts, minimal benefits, athletic facilities, educational assistance, employee discounts, cell phones from employer, meals, reimbursements for moving costs, retirement plan, transport, tuition reduction, working condition benefits, scholarships, and fellowships.

Remember the W2 form from the previous chapter? That is the form all the fringe benefits will be included on as taxable. The perks provided by the employer can vary from really attractive benefits, like rent or cars, to smaller ones. The benefits' value will be calculated according to their fair market value and costs on the market. The IRS also provides guidelines for calculating the value. Employers could be subject to high penalty fees if they fail to report all the benefits provided for their employees in the proper manner.

Capital Gains & Losses

Capital gains refer to profits a person earns when selling a capital asset,such as, property, stocks, shares, bonds, or mutual fund shares.

According to tax law, we have long-term and short-term capital profits. Short-term capital gains are defined as profits that you earn from selling an asset which has been in your ownership no longer than a year. Short-term capital gains can be very tricky when it comes to taxation.The highest tax rate is applied to this kind of sale, where you will have to pay a 43.3% rate. This might discourage you from selling newly acquired assets and wait until they reach long-term status.

Long-term capital gains are profits coming from sold assets that have been in your ownership for more than a year. They are significantly lower, with tax rates starting from 0%, 15%, or 20% for the last year.

We already mentioned the short-term gains maximum tax rate, which could be even liable to an additional surtax for Medicare up to almost 37%, but that depends on your income.

When it comes to taxed long-term gains, low tax payers (bracket 10/15%), can even hope for a 0% rate, while other tax payers will have to pay the 15% or 20% tax rate, unless otherwise exempted from it under tax law. Always take a look at exemptions in the tax law, because you may be in a tax-exempt category.

Real estate capital gains in depreciation come with a 25% tax rate unless you are a low tax payer (10 and 15% bracket).

Capital losses are defined as capital asset sale losses (e.g. stock, real estate, bond, mutual fund). Losses are also broken into short-term and long-term capital losses. Capital losses can generate deductions, and they are to be reported to tax authorities only if expected to rise in value. They can be reported to secure deductions on the tax return.

We also have realized & unrealized losses, as well as recognizable gains. Unrealized losses are not to be reported, and refer to losses where the asset you bought drops in value, but you do not sell it immediately. Instead, wait until its value increases again, and then sell it. You can only report when the actual sale happened, which is referred to as realized loss, (assuming that you still sold it under the price that you purchased it at).

Capital gains and losses are now filed on a new form that was introduced not so long ago by the IRS. The 8949 form facilitates the process, offering a comparison between gains and losses provided by investment companies. Capital losses give you the opportunity to get back at least some of your losses via tax returns, which is still something.

Traditional IRA (Internal Revenue Service) and Roth IRA

Many US citizens do not know which retirement account to use...so which one is better? The traditional IRA account or the Roth IRA account? Let us explain the difference between the two of them so you can decide which one would be right for you.

An individual retirement account can have an impact, not only on you, but also your family in terms defining your long-term savings.

The traditional IRA is suitable for all persons who earned incomes and are under the age of 70, whereas the Roth IRA comes with certain criteria that have to be met by an individual.

To contribute to a Roth IRA, your incomes have to be below a specified amount defined by the IRS. The amount can vary from year to year. The amount which makes you eligible also depends on your marital status and the way you earned that income. Usually, your incomes should be earned (e.g. work), and not a result of non-earning incomes such as rentals, investment.

How the IRS specifies the amounts and limits depends on the modified adjusted gross income.

Be aware that the numbers, i.e. specified amounts, can change. Single households, as well as head of households, must have an annual income lower than $116,000 to qualify for Roth, while in 2016, the amount was specified at less than $132,000, and we can only wait to see what it is going to be in 2017.

A married couple who filed jointly must have had an income lower than $183,000 in 2015, and less than $194,000 in 2016.

Separate filing of married couples was an option if their annual income was less than $10,000.

So, if you fall under any of the given categories, you can file for a Roth IRA contribution, but further on, the savings limits for retirement also depend on your age. Married and single persons under 50 can contribute $5,500 to their IRA Roth fund. In the case of a married couple, where one spouse is employed, and the other is not, it is still possible to set aside $5,500 for each.

For persons over 50, the same amount contribution applies, only with the addition that they can set aside another $1,000, which makes up for a $6,500 limit on total Roth contribution for persons from age 50 onwards.

Rental Income

Rental income, as already mentioned, is also subject to taxes. Renters should keep a record of their rental expenses, as well as landlords, including cost, income, and expenses. To keep it neat and organized, landlords may use spread sheets or software for finances which are mass-used these days. As a landlord, you should list property management commissions, cleaning, maintenance and repair expenses, advertisement expenses, real estate taxes and mortgage interest rate costs, security deposits, as well as utility costs, trash, etc. Bear in mind to list the price at which the apartment or house was bought, as well as annual depreciation of the real estate.

Losses from a rental property can also be used to squeeze out certain deductions since passive activity losses are deductible.

Rents do not always generate net profit since the rent fee usually covers the mortgage, repairs, property tax, and sometimes insurance. Once the property depreciation is added, it can turn out that landlord's expenses are higher than profits from renting. If the loss is $25,000 or more, the landlord can count on the passive activity limitations which are set at this exact amount, which means that the landlord cannot lose more than $25,000 within a tax year.

If you are a landlord and want to sell your property that you have rented so far, you need to know that it differs from selling your private house or apartment which you live in. It involves subtracting the cost basis from the selling price.

CHAPTER 10

WHAT DEDUCTIONS CAN BE CLAIMED?

As a taxpayer, of course, you want to know what taxes can be deducted to relieve at least of some of the tax burdens you have to carry on your shoulders year in and year out.

When it comes to **moving expenses deductions**, there are certainly some windows open for deduction when filing taxes. Mostly, persons who moved because of a change of job or starting a new job, as well as moving their business or starting a business in a new location, can ask for tax deductions, but certain criteria have to be met in order to so.

The IRS provides a test on their website where you can determine for yourself if you qualify for a deduction due to moving expenses. The test criteria are connected to the reasons for moving. If it is for work, you will definitely be able to request a deduction, but only if you, in addition, meet the distance criteria, (distance would be greater from your old home to the new job, over 50 miles), and the time criteria. The time criteria refers to your time of work, and as an employee, you should be working 39 weeks for the first year of your employment or starting of business, i.e. you have to be a full-time employee.

Members of the Armed Forces do not have to meet time and distance criteria since they move upon request of their superiors.

Moving expenses should also be listed on the appropriate form which is Form 3903. The IRS will decide which moving expenses can be deducted and mostly the following qualify as deductible:

• The cost of boxing up and transporting your household goods and personal effects

• The cost of shipping your car and your household pets

• Storage expenses

- Car transportation expenses

- Transportation expenses (other than car)

You may also file for **<u>charitable deductions</u>** if you contributed to a qualifying charity organization. The charity contribution may be in property or cash. The deductions can be as high as 50% of your adjusted gross income, but in some cases, it only reaches 20% or 30% (fraternal societies, veterans organizations, and cemetery organizations) which depends on the defined limitations. What organizations qualify for charity is another factor here, since there is an explicit list of what type of organization is eligible. They are:

- US or state-owned charity organizations for public purposes

- Trust funds, foundations, community chest, which were established under US laws for scientific, educational, religious, or literary purposes, and even those which refer to children and animal protection against cruelty

- Religious institutions, churches, synagogues, etc.

- War veterans trust funds, organizations within the USA or in its possession

- Fraternal societies limited to charitable purposes only

- Civil defense organizations

- Cemetery firms which are non-profit, and if the contribution was given for general maintenance of the cemetery, and not an individual grave

- Non-profit educational organizations (most of them)

- Non-profit research centers and hospitals

- Volunteer fire companies

You may also ask for a deduction if you have a US or foreign student living with you under a written agreement under a program of one of the qualified organizations who assist students in learning opportunities. The student may not be your relative and has to be a full time student.

As we said, the charity contributions should be paid in cash or property before the tax year expires in order to file for deduction.

Nevertheless, there are some hacks which can help you squeeze out more deductions from your income taxes. For example, expenses right out of your pocket, if they were spent for charitable work. Let's say you participated in a fund-raising action and made cookies for the purpose. Make sure to calculate the ingredient costs, which can be helpful in itemizing the costs if subject to an audit. Other out-of-pocket expenses which qualify are, for example, funding some activities for unprivileged children, (which again have to be part of a program of a qualified organization). The activities can include movie tickets you bought for them, dinner, or athletic events, etc.

If one of the organizations sends you to a convention, you may file for deduction on travel and lodging costs.

Persons would not qualify for charity contribution deductions if they made a contribution to a specific individual, non-qualified organizations, donor-advised fund, etc. They also can not ask for deduction for their time spent on a particular cause, personal expenses, appraisal fees, etc.

Casualty Loss Deductions

A casualty loss refers to property damage caused by natural disasters such as floods, earthquakes, tsunamis, etc. If the property is your personally used property, or if the property is only partly destroyed, your casualty loss amounts to less than the adjusted basis.If it is property you rent out or property that was completely destroyed, your loss will equal the adjusted basis.

Theft losses can also be deductible, and will amount to the adjusted basis of the loss due to theft, since the market value of the stolen asset equals zero after theft.

Both of the losses can be claimed as itemized deduction which requires you to fill out Form 1040.

Casualty deductions can be somewhat complicated since it depends on the ratio between your adjusted gross income and extent of the loss. You can only deduct if the loss exceeds 10% of the adjusted gross income. This means that if the loss is less than 10%, you will get nothing in deduction. You are also expected to minimize or reduce your loss by cashing-in from the insurance company which is supposed to reimburse you. The amount you receive from the insurance company further reduces casualty loss.

It is important to keep record of casualty losses, given the sensitivity of the topic, and the IRS will probably conduct an audit on that matter, so you better be prepared when filing for casualty loss deduction by making sure to have proof that the asset or property was in your ownership (e.g. receipt, agreement), as well as proof of the fair market value of the asset or property (repair costs, appraisal, etc.).

Claiming Deductions Based on Dependents

We already mentioned the dependent status, but now let us commit to the topic in terms of deductions. If you have a dependent person which you support with your income, then, you might be able to save thousands of dollars which otherwise would be taxed. Of course, there are several dependent categories which make you eligible to file for deduction. Qualifying children, parents, and relatives qualify as dependents. The dependent has to be a US, Canadian, or

Mexican citizen, as well as a person who is filing a joint return with his or her spouse (e.g. your married daughter files jointly with her husband). Otherwise, they do not qualify.

Children can be your own, step-children, adopted, and fostered and they must be under 19, or under 24 if full-time college students. Disabled children qualify regardless of their age. The child has to be living with you for at least six months. Also, children who work part-time, but whose incomes are not sufficient to make a living and depend on your income, qualify as dependents.

Parents and only a special list of relatives do not have to live with you to be listed as dependents. All other relatives, on the other hand, have to be members of your household to be eligible. Also, you have to be the only claimant of the relative, since no dependent can be claimed twice (or by two different persons).

CHAPTER 11

HOW MUCH IN TAXES DO YOU OWE?

If you are an employee, your income tax is usually regulated by your employer who sends the tax deductions to the IRS, meaning that you do not have to be responsible for that. Self-employed persons and those who make profit outside of their regular income could be liable to estimated tax payments. The extra incomes refer to interest income, dividends, selling stocks, business incomes, and alimony.

Paying your taxes on time is a rule of thumb, and if you withhold tax payment, you might be penalized by the IRS. In order to find out how much you owe, you need to make an estimate of your income and the deductions. Turbo Tax software is often used for this purpose, which can calculate your taxes accurately. Taking a look at your taxes from the year before is also a good idea, which will refresh your memory of what incomes and deductions you have to file.

The tax payment process is usually divided into four installments where you may or may not pay a fixed amount. This depends on whether you have withheld taxes or made a lot of money in a quarter, etc.

The Alternative Minimum Tax

The AMT is a mechanism that was developed to prevent rich taxpayers from not paying taxes. Exemption from AMT is automatically adjusted to inflation. The AMT was aimed at setting a clear minimum for all taxpayers, especially rich ones, who had avoided tax payments in the past by using deductions, which resulted in no taxes. This system is responsible for limitations in deductions. It is an additional tax to the regular tax. The tax makes up for all the exemptions and beneficial circumstances which granted lower payment of regular income taxes. In that way, it restores balance in the tax system.

Child Tax Credit

This credit can benefit your family as a whole since they can be worth up to $1,000 per child. The child tax credit reduces income taxes up to $1,000. To be eligible for this credit, your child has to be your dependent. There is only one difference, for a child tax credit, which is that the child has to be under 17. The amount of the tax credit also depends on your adjusted gross income, i.e. if it is above a certain amount, the child tax credit will be lower. The amount again depends on your status. When filing jointly as a married couple, the limit is $110,000, and for separate filing as a married couple, the limit starts at $55,000 of adjusted gross income. For single and other individuals, the phase-out starts at $75,000.

Still, this is not all, if you owe tax money, regular and alternative, that will also influence the amount of the child tax credit,. So make sure to have no debts towards the IRS. If it happens that the sum you owe in tax money is greater than the child tax credit, you can file for an additional child tax credit.

The Earned Income Tax Credit

The low and moderate-income earners can look forward to squeezing some money out of the Personal Credit or Earned Income Tax Credit. To obtain the credit, you have to file a tax return separately. Of course, some criteria have to be met to qualify for the personal credit. By filing this tax return, you have the opportunity to lower your usual tax payments and gain a refund.

Eligible persons are employees who work for an employer, as well as people who run or own their own business, including having a farm. If you are a worker with or without a qualifying child, some additional rules apply.

So your income, including your adjusted gross income, are not to exceed the specified amount defined by the IRS, basic rules have to be met, and you must comply with additionalrules if you have or have not a qualifying child.

If you are married, then one of the basic rules is to submit the social security numbers of you, your spouse, and a qualifying child if included on the list of your tax return. The social security number has to be issued before due data and validation of employment. Bear in mind, that this tax return cannot be filed separately if you are married, only when married and filing jointly.

Tax investment income for the year is not to exceed $3,400, however you also have to have registered income in the amount of at least $1 if your status is single, head of the household, or widower, and you have no qualifying children, your incomes can not be over $14,880 in order to qualify. If you have qualifying children, then the following applies:

1. Qualifying child- maximum income $39,296

2. Qualifying children- maximum income $44,648

3. More qualifying children- maximum income $47,955

If you are married and file jointly (which you have to do in order to to obtain the personal credit), the maximum income amount for a couple with no qualifying children is $20,430. If they have qualifying children, then the numbers are:

1. Qualifying child- maximum income $44,846

2. Qualifying children- maximum income $50,198

3. More qualifying children- maximum income $53,505

Please note, that these numbers are only valid for the last 2016 tax year and that they are subject to change. Still, they provide a good framework for giving you an idea on how the incomes have to look like to apply for a tax return for a personal credit.

Additional rules for qualifying children include the basics which we have already mentioned throughout the book; the child must meet the age criteria, live with you, and claimed by you. For persons with no qualifying children, the basic rules include residency in the USA for the past six months, you must be between the ages of 25 and 65, and you should not be claimed on somebody else's tax return. When it comes to qualifying children with disabilities, and special categories of people, like the military staff and clergy, disaster-affected and disabled persons, the IRS lowers the criteria.

Estimated Taxes

Estimated taxes are all those taxes that are not included in the regular withheld income reserved to regular taxes which most of the Americans pay as they go. So, regular taxes ae those that are automatically transferred to the IRS by our employers on our behalf. Estimated taxes are a special category which includes incomes from your own business (self-employed persons), dividend and interest rate incomes, capital gains, alimony, and prize money. Tax estimates also include income and alternative minimum taxes as well. They are usually paid on a quarterly basis, and they are mandatory. If you do not pay your share to IRS of the untaxed income you receive, you will be liable to penalties.

In order to avoid that, fill out the estimated tax Form 1040-ES which are also very convenient to calculate the estimated taxes. Do not forget that all American citizens are obliged to report estimated taxes, and they are your own responsibility, so you have to take care of it. Since the American tax system relies on regular tax payments, regular reports have to be submitted to the IRS including estimated taxes as well. According to the IRS, estimated taxes should be submitted four times a year.

The estimation should be made by calculating estimated taxes for the entire tax year, whereby you divide it by four to get the amount you need to pay on a quarterly basis. You can use the

IRS Form to calculate the amount, but you can also do it online via different finance calculators and software, such as TurboTax.

To make the calculation, you have to take into account the expected adjusted gross income, regular income subject to taxes, annual credits, and deductions via tax return. You can take a look at your estimated taxes from last year to figure out your deductions, etc.

All of this sounds simple, but many citizens delay the submission of estimated taxes and spend the cash without leaving aside for taxes, deceiving themselves that they will compensate the amount at a later stage. Such an approach can easily lead you to underpaying your taxes, which can result in fines and penalties if your debt in taxes reaches $1,000. Penalties will not be your only problem then, but you will also have to pay interest on the tax amount owed.

CHAPTER 12

STRATEGIES TO SAVE ON TAXES

Since the American tax system would be indeed rigorous without deductions and tax returns, it can be truly advantageous to find all the loopholes which enable you to save on taxes.

Incomes for selling your house normally refer to capital gains, which are taxable, of course, but there is a way to sell your home and circumvent the capital gain tax, which would be referred to as **Tax-Free Residence Sale**. Before 1997, taxes on property sale had to be paid only unless the seller bought a new home that was more expensive from that money within two years. Luckily, the Taxpayer Relief Act discontinued such a practice and enabled home-sellers a few tax benefits. Nowadays, if you sell your house for up to $250,000 and in some cases $500,000, you do not have to pay a dime to the IRS, since profit taxes are only incurred on larger amounts.

This tax break can only be used if you are selling your house you live in, i.e. your primary home; all other properties, like houses you rented out until you sold it, etc. These cases are treated as capital gain and will be taxed accordingly. The other criteria are the time requirement, i.e. you must have lived in that house for at least two years.

Investing in Securities

There are securities you can invest in that are not subject to taxes. This means that the interest earned on your securities assets is going to stay in your pockets. There are numerous debt securities which are offered to spur capital, and they are tax-exempt as well. They are the so-called municipal bonds, which can be tax-free on all three levels, (state-federal-local), as long as the securities holder lives in the state/city/area where the bond comes from. The most popular tax-free investments in this category are general obligation bonds and revenue bonds, which are aimed at financing government projects and others that are backed by the money made from the specific project. The statistics have shown that those who usually pay the highest taxes are more likely to invest in these tax-free bonds.

Since the bonds are tightly linked to interest rates and their movements, there is a certain risk investors have to enter. For example, if the interest rates move against your favor, you will earn less. Also, these bonds are not always liquid enough, which makes them harder to sell on the market if needed.

Nevertheless, every investment, whether it be in stocks or bonds, is risky anyways, so you might as well opt for a risk that relieves you from taxes.

Tax Credits for Education

There are two educational tax credits that can be used to cover higher education students' costs. These credits usually lower income taxes which result in more savings than from a simple tuition deduction. The first one is the American Opportunity Credit which relieves you from $2,500 tax payment per student. The student has to be attending one of the qualified universities of the federal student aid program. The credit is available for students from their first to their fourth year of college and is valid for one tax year. The student is also not to be registered as a drug felon. The credit usually covers tuition costs, educational resources like books, and equipment needed for the studies.

The other credit is the Lifetime Learning Credit, and anyone who pays taxes and attends one course minimum at a university which is a member of the federal student aid program can apply. The applicants do not have to pursue a certificate to be eligible, but simply be enrolled in one course. It covers tuition fees and book expenses, supplies, etc.

If you are a student or a person who claims a student as a dependent, hurry up and seize the opportunity to make some major cuts in tax payments by applying for one of the two credits. Make sure not to miss out on such a great opportunity.

Armed Forces

Being a member of the honorable American military grants you many advantages when it comes to taxes. This tax group enjoys some of the best tax breaks and benefits. For example, serving in a combat zone relieves you from paying any income taxes for the month or months you are out there. The IRS keeps a detailed list of qualified combat zones, so you might want to check them out.

Also, if married, military staff does not have to be present when filing jointly. Your spouse can simply submit it with a power of attorney. The military, usually changing stations frequently, has the right to reimbursement via special deduction rules for the military.

Also, military members who are returning to civilian life and are looking for a job can file for special deductions to cover costs of travel and other fees, which they are obliged to pay while seeking employment. Since the military tax rules can be confusing, the IRS offers free tax assistance to military members and their families free of charge so they can help with filing for deduction, exemption, etc.

CHAPTER 13

PLANNING IDEAS FOR YOUR BUSINESS

If you want to open your own business, you probably have already thought about the taxes that come along with it. So it is good to know where you can save money, especially in taxes. Let us see what you can count on as a self-employed taxpayer.

Home Office Deduction

It is as simple as it sounds. Open the office in your home and you can file for deduction for some business expenses. The criteria you have to meet are not that difficult. To qualify for a home business deduction, you simply have to use a premise at your home exclusively for business conducted on a regular basis. Another criterion is that your home is your principal seat of business from where you run all business operations. If you are a small business owner who conducts their business inside and outside the home, i.e. at two locations, you can still file for deduction for the expenses incurred at your home as a workplace.

The home space used for business has to be submitted in percentage, so you should calculate what percentage of your home is used for your business. The home office deduction can also be used by employees who work for an employer from their own home.

Keogh, Simple, or SEP

Small business retirement plans might not be the favorite part of small business owners, but it is a little bit easier on them when they know that at least some tax benefits are included for each retirement plan.

Keogh, Simple, or SEP retirement plans are known for various tax breaks, and are favored by American small business owners.

The Simple IRA is a plan designed for employees and allows them to make their own contributions. The employer makes the contribution plan for individual retirement accounts. The contribution limits for this plan are the lowest when compared to other plans, and an employer must count 100 employees to be eligible for the Simple IRA. Employees do not have to pay regularly, but the employer has to (from 1% to 3%). The limit is set at slightly above $12,000 for now, and it might be raised again. Persons over the age of 50 can apply for a catch-up contribution in the amount of additional $3,000.

Under the **SEP Plan,** all employees have to receive the same benefits. The contributions are deductible, which means that employers and employees can count on breaks in income taxes. This plan requires employers to withhold 25% of the employees' income and put it in their SEP account. Self-employed persons have a lower limit that is approximately 18.6% of net profit.

Keogh Plan

The main benefit of a Keogh Plan for the self-employed is that the contribution limits are far higher than for the other two. This retirement plan is still not as mainstream as the other two, and the administrative procedure is far more demanding. Contributions are made before taxes are paid which makes them eligible for the deduction for that year, but the main setback is that later when retired, you will be required to pay taxes on that money upon withdrawal. Withdrawals are only allowed when a person turns 59 ½, and all prior withdrawals could end up in penalties.

The employers and employees have to make detailed calculations in order to find out which retirement plan works out best for them, as well as which will grant them the best tax benefits. Not all citizens are in the same position, and one plan might work for one individual, but not for the other, and vice versa.

There is also an open window for deduction on the business use of cars. Simply calculate the car expenses by standard mileage rate or real-time expenses you had to pay and file for a deduction. The requirements are pretty simple, and almost every self-employed person can apply, but to be sure, check out the special requirements on the IRS website.

Self-Employment Tax basically refers to social security and Medicare taxes. To calculate self- employment taxes, the IRS provides Form 1040. The percentage of the tax rate for this tax has been reduced since 2012, and in 2016 it was 15.3% for $11,850 of net income, whereby 2.9% are additionally incurred on net incomes exceeding $11,850.

CHAPTER 14

NOW THAT YOU ARE DONE...

Finally, we are coming to the end of our tax guidebook, and there are only a few things left to explain. Now that we are done with the basics let us take a quick look at penalties and tax extensions, amended returns, and IRS audits.

Tax Penalties

We already have mentioned tax penalties throughout the book and warned you about when it comes to such an unfortunate event. So let us quickly review what has been said.

You can count on the IRS to penalize you in the case of late payments and late filing. The deadline is April 15th, also called the Tax Pay Day. Until this date, you are supposed to have paid all taxes you owe. Make sure to file your taxes by the given date, as well as to be tax-clear byApril 15th each year.

If you cannot meet your tax obligations, you are still obliged to file, and by doing so, you will avoid penalties and will be able to cover your tax debts by paying from your tax return money. As long as you are honest with the IRS, everything should be fine. For example, you can make an agreement to pay in installments.

The failure-to-pay penalty is incurred on you when you failed to pay your taxes, and it amounts to ½% of 1% of the unpaid taxes.

If you have regularly paid 90% of your taxes, you can ask for an extension for filing (on time of course), where the IRS will not fine you with the failure-to-pay penalty, but will expect you to pay the remaining amount you owe.

Filing an Extension

The IRS provides the opportunity for all late payers and late filers to ask for a 6-month extension before they submit their tax return. The best part about this is that it is granted almost automatically with no particular criteria, as long as you sent your extension request in a timely manner with the appropriate form. But, make sure to check the laws applicable in your state, since some states have separate extension request forms. You can submit online via Form 4868, but also in hard copy by the deadline. Asking for an extension is free and easy with no further complications. After the IRS grants you the following six months, make sure to calculate all relevant tax data and all incomes to make your tax return more efficient. It is always better to file an extension than to pay unnecessary penalty fees due to failure to file.

Amended Returns

Amended returns are not obligatory at all. Still, if you are filing an amended return, you must be aware that it means that you have to correct all entries. You cannot just make changes to those aspects that bring you back your money, as well as those that might increase your taxes. Form 1040X is the form to be used to file for amended return, and can be filed only in hard copy, not electronically.

Some people file for amended tax return due to mathematical mistakes, but there is no need to bother with that since the IRS will already catch up on and rectify these mistakes themselves. The deadline for filing amended returns is three years from the date you submitted the original return. Filing an amended return might result in a more advantageous tax return so it is definitely worth it when you know you could squeeze something out of it.

IRS Audit

There are some factors that could trigger the IRS to knock on your door. Even if chances are small, since this happens only once in a blue moon, we will discover what could lead the IRS to pay you a visit.

If you happened to earn a million during the tax year, you would probably be eligible for an IRS audit. Usually, the wealthy elite are the IRS target since they want to make sure that everything is in line with the law.

The second case that qualifies for an IRS audit is if you overdid it with charitable deductions. If you happen to give away more to charity than you earn, you might expect the IRS to show up at your door.

Estate tax returns are also a weak point for the IRS, especially if the estate is larger than average. They might take a second look at what you have been up to. Also, if you fail to report all of your income, you will be subject to audit. The best thing is, especially if you make money on the side, to keep a detailed record of all your earnings to avoid slippage in reporting.

Make sure to avoid major errors in tax filing, and please note, that you should never withhold a payment on purpose, since the IRS is known for finding out every irregularity. Rely on this book to use all the tax advantages and tax breaks and do not engage in illegal activities. Remember that as long as you cooperate with the IRS, they cooperate with you.

CONCLUSION

Now that you have finished reading through this book, my hope is that you have learned some useful information regarding both federal and state taxes in the United States. You should now know where income taxes originated and where all of your tax dollars go. You should be aware of all the ways that you are taxed, as well as the different ways you can minimize what taxes you are paying. You should also have a basic understanding of corporate tax law and the different ways businesses are taxed.

From here, you can share the knowledge that you have with your family and friends, with enough sharing, we can help minimize the number of people who are oblivious to what our tax dollars are for. While it is annoying to have to give up a portion of your pay, knowing where that money is going can make it seem less of a hindrance. You can also take what you have learned and apply it to your life to be able to minimize the amount of income tax you are paying and increase the number of deductions you can claim on your income tax return.

I would like to thank you again for taking the time to download and read my book *"Taxes: Beginners Guide To Understanding Taxes And Why We Pay Them."* I hope you found this book to be a beneficial learning tool and now have a better understanding of taxes.

FREE BONUS: "Click The Link Below To Receive Your Bonus

https://publishfs.leadpages.co/pangea-health/

FREE BONUS: "Click The Link Below To Receive Your Bonus

https://publishfs.leadpages.co/pangea-health/

References

"Taxpayer Advocate Service - Taxpayer Bill of Rights." Taxpayer Advocate Service. IRS.gov, July 2014. Web. 24 Oct. 2016. Publication 5170 (7-2014) Catalog Number 66849X